POSTS AND PROMISES

Bro. Jon Briggs

WESTBOW
PRESS®
A DIVISION OF THOMAS NELSON
& ZONDERVAN

Copyright © 2015 Bro. Jon Briggs.

All rights reserved. No part of this book may be used or reproduced by any means, graphic, electronic, or mechanical, including photocopying, recording, taping or by any information storage retrieval system without the written permission of the author except in the case of brief quotations embodied in critical articles and reviews.

WestBow Press books may be ordered through booksellers or by contacting:

WestBow Press
A Division of Thomas Nelson & Zondervan
1663 Liberty Drive
Bloomington, IN 47403
www.westbowpress.com
1 (866) 928-1240

Because of the dynamic nature of the Internet, any web addresses or links contained in this book may have changed since publication and may no longer be valid. The views expressed in this work are solely those of the author and do not necessarily reflect the views of the publisher, and the publisher hereby disclaims any responsibility for them.

Any people depicted in stock imagery provided by Thinkstock are models, and such images are being used for illustrative purposes only.
Certain stock imagery © Thinkstock.

ISBN: 978-1-5127-0965-0 (sc)
ISBN: 978-1-5127-0966-7 (e)

Library of Congress Control Number: 2015913755

Print information available on the last page.

WestBow Press rev. date: 9/4/2015

This is dedicated to my family, my friends and everyone that needs a nudge in the good direction from time to time. I hope my situations and resolutions can help in a simple way. His way. I hope you understand.

Brother Jon

The artwork in the pages of this book was created by Rachel Prince, a college student who attends Highland Chapel Union Church where I pastor. A talented and beautiful child of God. Thanks Rachel!

Thank You Kimberly Birdwell for the beautiful photographs used on the cover! They are terrific!

5-19-15

Impressions. What a part of life. Good ones, bad ones, false ones, then changing them, soliciting them, debating them, understanding them, misunderstanding them, sharing them, keeping them to ourselves and on and on and on. For a believer so many times folks are gathering their impressions of us. Me for instance, I'm not perfect by any means. It's only by God's love and grace and mercy and understanding that I have hope and happiness, and willing to share. When no one else understands me or has a flawed impression of me, He really knows me. With so many people in our worlds, we worry about the impressions we leave. We usually do get a second chance with family and true friends. His impression of us is accurate and perfect. Kinda humbling don't you think. I am thankful. Very, very thankful that we can trust Him. When we do, it sure leaves an eternal impression. Hope you understand. I needed that.

5-21-15

Prayer time. Let's see, need to remember BB, Jess, kids, sis, aunts, uncles, cuzes, friends and church folks. Special requests, S and S in Northcrest, W at home, E in Centennial, the B family and the M family. EMS, PD, FD, soldiers, church folks. leaders and followers, other well people and not well people, the lost and the found, sad/happy, lonely, content, needy, not so needy. Well He knows the needs. Best part is I'm fairly certain that someone's praying for me. Is that not cool? We pray, they pray, we all pray. That's that love one another thing, yep, that's what that is. If you don't think He even knows your name, I assure you He does, He really does and loves you beyond measure... right where you are, praying or not, He is there. Hope you understand. Of course that's another prayer......

5-7-15

Just spent some time with a sweet family that have given up a husband, father, grandfather, great-grandfather, brother, uncle and friend. Over time I've figured out that when a brother or sister in Christ (and that includes family and friends) goes home they experience the presence of God Himself and have a new perspective in that they, at that moment, that second, have absolute knowledge of how true the promises of God really are. Being there allows no doubts for those that are already there that He can, does and will keep His promises to us. I find great comfort in that myself. Our Lord is faithful and true. I felt the need to share this. Thank you all for being my family and friends. I am a blessed man.

5-16-15 Class of 74.

We went to kindergarten in 1961 it was our turn, first grade in 62, 8th grade in 69-70, then graduated in 1974. We voted and figured out what we wanted to do in life, taking what we believed and finally applied it to our life, we figured out how to make a living... it was our turn each time. Then we married somebody, some had kids, it was our turn again. Then the kids had kids, grandparents we became because it was our turn. We are getting ready to retire because it's our turn. Now the grandkids are graduating from I guess everywhere they can graduate from these days... now it's their turn. The interesting thing is we got to take our turns and then take their turns with them... icing on the cake of life. Groovy when you think about it. I pray all this year's graduates enjoy their turn, it last's a lifetime.... Congratulations!

5-5-15

Healing is a wonderful fact of life. Each of us heals in different ways because we all hurt differently. We all carry some kinda scars, on the outside and on the inside. We all have tears that come, whether seen by others or just Jesus. There are times when the healing doesn't come the way we want it to or when we want it to or how we want it to, but it comes. When Jesus took our blame His suffering physically, emotionally and mentally was very real and that is the way we are healed. Through His suffering. Kind of preachy but the truth is His grace is perfected in our weakness, no matter what it is....grace is the foundation of our healing. All because He loves us. Never forget that you are loved, you may not think so but you really, really are. He knows us, everyone. Hope you understand... love one another.... that's good stuff....

4-22-15

God is good. He understands stuff we don't. He loves us regardless of what we look like, sound like and act like for the most part. He made us all different, a gazillion people, created in His image. Free to choose who, what, where, why etc as we go thru life. Even in the great times and not so great times we choose. How we're going to be. top to bottom, front to back as we change moment to moment, thought to thought, mood to mood, emotion to emotion. We need to choose to trust Him and lean on His promises. He speaks to us. The Spirit nudges us along. His Son was, is and will always be. Yes, He does understand the stuff we don't, that's why He won't ever leave us or forsake us...Yes God is good.... all the time.

4-18-15

"Passage" is an interesting word for me. Yesterday one of our dear friends had a passage from this place we call home to the place God made to be our eternal home. It's sad and our hearts hurt for his family, his friends and ourselves. God also gave us His Word and passages from His Word will bring us to another place, a little beyond today and even the next few days, but the transition will be there. Passages; a prayer and a promise, hand in hand will protect our hope and bring us peace for a while, until the next person's passage arrives. I'm always mindful of Faith, Hope and Love. Love is the greatest. Embracing Love is a wonderful gift to have for a passage. Hope you understand. Pray for our church family and my friends.

4-14-15

The day is done, said my prayers and ready to turn in. I want a full night's sleep. So in anticipation of one, I'm sitting here thinking about what I want to dream. Don't want some vampire, neck chewing sleep vision in stereo, that's for certain. Don't want to dream about food. Makes me wake up hungry if I remember. Don't want to have a claustrophobic dream, you know stuck in an elevator, stuff like that....nope... Tonight I'd like to dream about fishing and talking and singing and laughing and listening and watching the kids jump and laugh and play. Maybe I could just dream about sleeping...now there's a concept. a dream about dreaming, But the dream of dreams is the dream that you have, you can't remember but your heart is smiling when you wake up. Kind of like heaven. Our eyes haven't seen nor our ears heard what our Father has in store for us in heaven but you know it's gonna be perfectly forever great with Him.... good thing about heaven is you can't sleep thru it. That's pretty cool.

4-3-15

Please go to church somewhere this Sunday whether you are out of the habit or out of touch. There is nothing quite like knowing we're loved, wanted and have hope no matter what. He knows your name, your life and your heart. The rest is up to us. It's real you know. Don't let anyone tell you that Jesus was just another one of some god's sons. He is the Living God's Only Son. He proved it. I believe it. I'll be in church Sunday. Me and my imperfections and His mercy. Hope you understand.

3-28-15

Just got back from eating out w/ BB, we had a very good meal at one of our favorite places. We had an even better conversation. You know the taste of the food will pass. The conversation we began didn't end however it just faded into normal. That's the way love is too. It has beginnings and re-beginnings but doesn't end. Love simply ebbs and flows with the rhythm of life. God's love seems that way, but it's constant. We move. I hope you understand... Love is the most powerful, wonderful, fearful, enjoyable, gracious, relieving feeling we can have, whether ebbing or flowing, coming in or going out. Sometimes love can fade, in good times or in bad times. Our appreciation for the real loves in our lives should just blend with our hearts, a permanent, influential, warm part of who we are ....you know? Have a great Sunday and come see us at HCUC when you can.... Blessings.

3-23-15

I'm kinda tired, doubt you ever get too tired. There's just so much to do, and so far behind, all that stuff ahead, just boggles the mind to get a hold of some of that stuff that is to be done, there to be done, could be done or might be done. Of course I just need to do one thing at a time, do it well, then what's behind moves forward a little and what's ahead aint' too far away, both directions get a little closer to where I am so I don't have to go too far either way to catch up or get ahead, God does take care of me. He's ahead of me making the path, sorting out what's behind me, you know that stuff I gave up on or I've passed up or passed on.... you know if I'll just wait on Him I'll get a recharge for the things I have in my life to do. Hope sure does help us with that tired thing sometimes better than a good nap, just letting go for a while and letting God be in our lives...sometimes we all need to work on that, I can do that and do it well, just need to do it more often and I wouldn't be so tired sometimes ... wow, I feel better just saying it... don't think preachers have it all figured out, we still like to " get tired "...... hope you understand.

3-17-15

What to pray for? Lord knows more about stuff than I do. He listens to what is about to be said, reaches out to those who are lifting their hands, lends His touch to those whose hearts are full and loves us all when we don't think we're loveable. His presence is the power from which we find our faith, so thanksgiving and praise are prayerworthy. New word prayerworthy. Yes that's what we pray for, all things prayerworthy, I can't think of anything or anyone that's not.....I guess I do know what to pray for.... He is good!

3-15-15

Monday is coming, what will it bring you? happiness, sadness, riches, losses, good news, bad news, new direction, wrong turns, light, darkness, laughter, a few tears, new adventures, complacency, answers, questions, more, less, healing, discomfort, hassles, peace. Yes Monday will be here shortly. I will meet my Monday with the attitude of trusting in God no matter what, seeking Him, listening to Him, talking WITH Him. Monday is coming, He's already here. Hope you understand,

3-10-15

Blessings from " Afar "... some things to consider: the weather yesterday evening was damp/drizzly and cool. What ever happened in that garage happened quickly. We heard the fire engine and RPD arrive (interesting emotion when they don't keep going) looked and then stepped outside, cool and wet, saw the glow and pretty much knew it was either the garage or a mobile home next door. as the fire was probably building steam (no pun I assure you) the Greenbrier FD and White House Community FD were training as I understand, were basically ready to go when the call came, climbed in and were on the way. When I went around to see the inferno this little building had become, the rock facia on our Christian Life Center was hot to the touch. vinyl soffit and siding were melting and some falling, The doors were hot to the touch. I basically froze in prayer, ever do that? Funny feeling, God knew the emotions of my heart as the water began flowing and they had this 30 ft tall fire/beast knocked down in short order. Ridgetop FD was on site almost immediately, using their tower (yes Ridgetop needed this and got it) to protect and otherwise prevent further damage from the immense heat this fire generated. All was cooled down with a steady flow from the hose and steady light rain from heaven.. One TV station miss reported that HCUC had burned down. Our building was never on fire on the outside. But we enjoy the " fires of love, trust and spirit " on the inside. We did last night too. The outpouring of love, friendship and prayers from our brothers and sisters is another story altogether. Humbled and amazed I am. Yes we can surely count our blessings from "Afar". I love you guys, we're going to be better than OK. But then that's how God is,

2-28-15

What's on my mind. Normal is returning here from winter. Today there is a wedding at our church, a new beginning for a young man and young woman. They'll make promises, take vows and celebrate with their families. A special time. What's on my mind. Normal is still away for some friends of mine. A funeral today, sickness, treatments, transitions, loneliness, uncertainty, frustrations ; all of these and more. Life does have peaks and valleys. God provides us with the ultimate support group. He is the leader, Christ His son the way maker, the Holy Spirit the comforter, His Word a light, His angels, our family and friends. But then since he's made provision, I guess normal includes the unexpected and unknown. As the song says, Prayer is the key, but faith unlocks the doors of life.

2-19-15

Prayer is on my mind. Not when to pray or how to pray. Not where to pray or even why to pray. It's Who I pray to, who I pray for and the measure of faith I've been given. Leo and Ken are friends of mine that need my prayers, as do Joel and Denise and Holly's family. Tylor's right in there along with many others that I know and care about. Most important is how He hears me. Behind the words and between the lines of thought He knows the entire circumstance. Even better than I do and I know, boy do I know that He loves them, all of them, each one that's on my list and in my heart and mind. If you're out of practice here's a clue...."Our Father, Who are it heaven, may your name be holy and honored", now you've ramped up and are ready to go.... share your heart, He wants us to.... hope you understand.

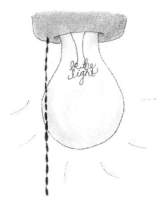

2-11-15

Gonna do " Turn on the Light, Part Two" Sunday morning. I feel I need it. The other day I was down, very unusual for me to be down, but I was. I just couldn't shake the blue/blahs. That was part of my inspiration for reading Ps 119:105. There are so many " lights " in His Word that they are easy to find, easy to read . Not easy to get with it, when you're down. You gotta want to turn it on and even if you do get into the Light you have to be willing to " look ". Lamp unto my feet and Light unto my path, right, so when we open our eyes, He opens our hearts, so we can see the light. Oh me, glad I saw where I was going... and not traveling with the blue/blahs is a great gift. Hope you understand.

2-7-15

It's Saturday again. Breakfast will be in a little while, some shopping, spending time with family. Also prayerfully going over my sermon in my heart. " Turn on the Light ". Psalms 119: 105 tells us that His Word is a light for our feet so we can see up close and our path so we can see where He's taking us. It's interesting when the stuff of life comes at us and we just falter, forgetting to " turn on the Light " in our lives. It's all in there, in His Word you know. so when you're lifting your prayers, reach for the Light. Probably got a copy of the Light laying around pretty handy.....

1-31-15

It's Saturday morning. Thank the Lord for the day ahead. He answered my prayers yesterday. Not all my way but all His way. The more I learn about life, the more I do trust Him. Being human isn't easy is it? He made us. We are in His pastures. The still waters belong to Him. Surely goodness and mercy will follow me today and tomorrow so I can stay with Him forever when I do go home. Makes me happy to know I'm loved like that. Bring on today...

1-27-15

Tuesdays, they seem kind of harmless, they are important. They can be another Monday or can be a new day. Usually that's our choice I believe. Usually. Then we might try something different to make sure Tuesday isn't another Monday. But then wonder why are Mondays so rough? We have to give ourselves up to take care of ourselves and ours. For a job. Thankful that we have Mondays. Our eternity is the same. We have to give ourselves to God on His terms to take care of ourselves and what's ours. For a promise. Once we do, He is in charge and that's when every Monday and Tuesday and all the rest of those days belong to Him. Thankful that little is much, when He is in it. Tomorrow is Wednesday... really looking forward to Wednesday!

1-24-15

We're back on line. Tomorrow's sermon focus is from the 23rd Psalm. Yea though I walk through the valley of _____, I will fear no evil, for He is with me. Fill in the blank, say a prayer and trust, always. Oh yeah, don't use your understanding, no matter what. We are loved.

1-16-15

I heard a very wise young man speak today. He spoke from the heart because he understands " stuff ". He's lived "stuff " as we all have. He challenged us all to give Jesus our " stuff ". As I listened to his words of fact I was humbled again by the spirit in me. In my eyes I still have " stuff ". In Jesus eyes I don't have " stuff " anymore. He gave me the gift of taking my "stuff ". Think about it. Ain't no "stuff" too tough for Him. He resisted " stuff " when He was a young man. Yeah, Jesus got our " stuff " and we got grace. And that's good stuff....for us all....

1-14-15

No matter what " what or it " is, God is. No matter where what or it is, God is. No matter when what or it happens, God is. No matter to whom what or it happens when or where, God is. He's really good at " is ".... you know?

1-10-15

Over the course of several weeks I've had interactions with many people from many walks of life. Some have a course which was set at some point in their lives, moving daily toward our Father. Some have chosen to not move in His direction. Some want to make the right turn towards the Father and just don't know how, or think they're not worthy or that they are too late. Make the turn you need to make, remind yourself that one of the thieves crucified with Jesus was in paradise that day with Him. Think about Lazarus, Jesus got there 4 days late by Mary and Martha's witness and yet Lazarus lived. I guess I'm sharing hope. Hope comes from being loved. Love from the Father. From the Father through the Son. If you're looking for direction again, just go home, home to your family of faith. You'll find what you're looking for. Don't mean to preach to the choir here. It's good where the heart is. Thanks for listening.

1-8-15

Another day is almost done. Glad God created days and nights. Glad He created us too. We can share His light, care for each other and live and breathe and move in Him as we go through each day and night. I've had a good day. It's been a very good day. Days are not perfect usually, but today was close. Tonight I'll study Lamentations 3. Saying my prayers. Awed, humbled, respectful and loved with a perfect love, His. When no one else understands us, He does. He is faithful and true. Everyday His love is new and His light gets a little brighter. Yes, He did good today. Another day is almost here...

1-1-15

2015- I look forward to the opportunities we will have, the blessings ahead and our victories in life as well as the tough times we all endure. The Father takes us through them, not just to them. I only look back with respect and learning as we move through life together as family and friends. Little IS much when He is in it. It's a new day, a new year, fresh eyes and hearts if we choose them. Let's BE in 2015. All the best to everyone this year!

12-25-14

Well, the trash can is full. The clothes closet is full. The sock drawer is full. The refrigerator is full, the kid's toy boxes are full. And my tummy is full... AND most important my heart is so full. Full of love and blessings and most of all gratitude to my Father. His love is my greatest gift... with Him its Christmas every day. I sure hope you understand. Hope you're full!

12-14-14

Let there be peace on earth, let it begin in me; Peace in our hearts, in our homes, in our land. There is so much more love than hate, compassion than punishment, trust than mistrust, I will strive to be a good friend, neighbor and Godly in every roll in life I have. I will embrace the threads of life I share with others and rejoice. I refuse to magnify the moments of conflict and judgment of others resulting in strife and suffering. It's not my job. Forgiveness is not an option. Yes peace does begin with me and I will pray it forward.

12-8-14

8:37pm.

How should we make someone happy this Christmas? Little kids usually know what they want... games, dolls, motorcycles, toys and all that stuff that dreams are made of....yes that an easy one. Big kids just want a little love, doesn't take much and that is the stuff that dreams are made of for many. Just to hear someone's kind voice say " Merry Christmas ", we care for you. Now there's an opportunity. Random voices of kindness just sharing the spirit of life our Father gives us. No money needed. If you're not sure, pray it Forward...that will surely result in a moment of life and love. Christmas times a'coming!

12-4-14

9:52pm.

Sunday's Sermon: "Surely He is the Son of God!". They knew it back then, some denied Him back then. We know it now. Some still don't. I know because He lives in my heart. Matthew 27:51 pretty much covers it. BTW Christ is NOT a character in a fairy tale. Christmas is when Christians celebrate our greatest gifts: Faith, Hope and Love. All are in and of and through Christ Jesus. I hope you understand. Wish I could afford a billboard, I can't but I can show and share and "Pray it forward". Now there's an idea.

11-10-14

Such tragedy, care, turmoil, confusion, shock, disappointment, bewilderment, trials, concern, worry, wonder, fear, loss, hurt, tears, words, prayers, more prayers, love reaching down, hope, wonderful hope, healing, patience, love, Holy companionship, peace, rest, faith. Over time I'm in there somewhere and think many others are too. We have some serious knee time requiring our attention and devotion. He understands when we don't. Love one another, in His presence. Can't give up on God, He'll be there in that moment, no matter which one it might be. This has been on my heart for several weeks....time to share.

11-25-14

7:56pm.

Thank You Lord, just because of who You Are: My hope, friend, my tomorrow, my today, our deliverer, comforter, keeper of the heart, provider, forgiver, finisher of my faith, forever present, our mansion builder- surely providing the eternal reality of my decision to follow Him. Rock, Shepard, King. Much to be thankful for!, very much. No matter how comfortable or uncomfortable your Thanksgiving is this year, Count the good stuff and the not so good stuff. He's earned our gratitude...Gave His All...pray, enjoy, share and just "be "....Happy Thanksgiving.

11-13-14

9:13pm.

I will pray for several families that have suffered greatly in recent days. I do not know why bad things happen to good people, but they do. I'm praying for our Highland Chapel Union Church Mission Team as they leave in the morning for Phelps KY to take warmth and food to many in need there. I pray for those that answer the call when trouble makes its way into our worlds. And I will thank Him just because of Who He Is. would you join me? Even if you don't pray this sure would be a good time to start. It's not that difficult once you get started. Might take a while though. He is good.

11-5-14

8:44pm.

The least we can do? What is that? For who? When? Where? For the least of "these". Elections are over, many, many trains of thoughts and opinions are floating around. I think we need to keep trying, just to find a way to make a difference in the lives of others, not talking relief here, just a little love, kindness and time, If I can't figure out how to share it, live it and give it, I know that God will grant what I need to do what He wants me to do, the strength to be where He wants me to be and the hope to share who He really is. Trusting Him, the least I can do.

10-29-14

11:23pm.

Smile, laugh, relax, rest, renew. morning, new day, preparations, opportunities, goals, encounters. Closer walks, more open prayers, open heart, a touch from heaven, celebrate, smile, laugh, relax, rest........

10-18-14

9:47pm.

Forgiveness. It's really only a concept until we are truly forgiven...forever....for everything....by our Father....in heaven...holy is His name....wonderful, shepherd. Alpha, Omega, Lord....I love the way you love....even me....cause I need you. Yes I do. He's not waiting on our perfection to move in our lives, he's waiting for us to move to Him so he can heal our hearts and keep us with him...forgiven.....hope you know what I'm talking about.

10-11-14

I officiated a wedding ceremony this afternoon, a beautiful service for two wonderful friends. Such a precious expression of love. This was a new beginning for these two which will last a lifetime. Tomorrow afternoon I've been asked to play for a home going for a special friend, at the same time yet another family very special to me will gather to do the same for their mom. I got to thinking about it...there will be loving people to lead each service, beautiful expressions of love and respect for my wonderful friends. This will be a new beginning for these two who left us... which will last forever. I believe God for sure knows what He's doing. We just need to let Him do it. Hope you understand.

10-1-14

7:37pm.

Website asks " What's on your mind ?" I could sometimes fill a newspaper with all I have on my mind....one thing to another to another. Sometimes it's one thing. A big thing. Sometimes it's good sometimes it not good. Interesting thought is that their question isn't original. Our Father wants to know what's on our mind. As we think each thought, take each step, laugh each laugh and cry each tear....you know He wants to hear from us, ever thought He already knows....ain't that cool... but that's Him. Hope you understand.

9-22-14

You know obedience to what God wants is fairly easy (don't lie, steal, cheat, covet, dishonor etc... even not having any other gods in your life) when you think about it. OH but there's that odd one.... that love one another....how? Conditionally or without condition?....like He loves us or as we choose to define love?....do we forgive as we're forgiven? Yep for the most part the first 10, most of us are good.... but all need to work on that love one another commandment. Jesus told us about that one Himself..... seems simple enough... love one another....got faith, got hope, got love.... yes love is the greatest! I love being loved. Let someone know you care. Hope you understand. Have a good week!

9-17-14

So many thoughts tonight...dear friend has gone home to our Jesus. Family so sweet and caring. Another dear friend of mine got good news from a marrow biopsy. Family so sweet and caring. Still yet other friends who's grandchild is having to endure what many children must, and many others don't. Families so sweet and caring. The stress of my day pales in comparison. So glad my heavenly Father counts me as His. That's real good, so I have family and friends that are most caring...believe you do too....blessings are to be embraced and then counted... a fact of faith.

9-14-14

8:13pm.

Pray for the people I have on my heart please. God knows who they are and what they have and what they need and where they are and why I'm asking. He's good that way you know. Thanks my friends. Most of all thank you Lord. You are on Facebook too.....that might worry some folks if they knew I guess.

8-10-14

7:00pm.

Divine Appointments. This coming Sunday's sermon thought from the Book of Acts. These are for God's handiwork for our own lives and for His handiwork in the lives of those we can reach for, touch and care about....remember when someone reached for you? A Divine Appointment. Sometimes no matter how hard it might seem we can keep these. Can't miss one of these you know. Time is in His hands and He does make all things beautiful for His children.... in His time...Ever had a Divine Appointment? I sure have and know there are more to come. That's so good of Him to handle that....time. Have a good rest of the week.

8-12-14

When someone leaves us and goes to God, it's not up to us to judge that person. When the tears have dried the memories and laughs begin to call from yesterday, those are gifts that God grants us. Cherished not forgotten, appreciated as they were made to be. He did that so it's our job to trust Him and love each other no matter what. After all it is what matters, having Him in our hearts and sharing him with our hearts. Don't think I don't smile after a tear or two. Hope you understand.

8-6-14

8:55pm.

Eph.4:32. Kindness, I sure would love to see more of that. Love, I sure would love to find more of that. Profoundly He showed us the how, when and why. Gotta try harder. Hope you join me.

7-28-14

9:24pm.

What are we? Fearfully and wonderfully made. Who are we? Children of God. Where are we? Abiding in His creation. Why are we? Because God wanted us to be. When will we? In the twinkling of an eye. How did He? He could and He did and He does and He will. That's love and that's who He is.

7-23-14

8:09pm.

How did you start your day? How will you end your day? Was this your day or someone else's? If you don't pay much attention to how you start and end each day, you don't know what you're missing, because the best is in the middle: thankfulness, humbleness, accomplishment, laughter, love and mercy. Oh yeah, He made days.... that's cool.

7-20-14

8:37am.

Just gotta have a little faith, every day, every opportunity. Little is a lot when God is in it, no matter what "it" is.

7-9-14

8:05pm.

Understand and know our Father in heaven. Doing so will align your perspectives, priorities, passions, purpose and place in life...and don't forget His righteous paths, His peace, patience, power, precepts, presence and all His promises, promises to us, that's you and I. That's good stuff I do believe. As I grow older each day, I learn more each day so I can keep trusting while I'm adjusting. Hope you understand.

6-27-14

10:01pm.

1. This Sunday our church folks are going to sing all morning! Come be with us at Highland Chapel Union Church, Ridgetop TN

2. July 4th, around 5 PM. we'll have dogs, burgers and we'll do some boston butts on charcoal. folks will bring the rest...THEN we're going to pick and sing some more. Harmony and hominy, Banjo's, trios, apple pie and you are welcomed. We may pass the hat for the building program....

3. Wherever you are, thank God for the freedoms we have, His presence in our lives to face the future and for the song in our hearts. You have one, don't need to be Pavarotti or Vestal Goodman...just sing the song He gave you. It's for Him anyway...Good stuff!

6-23-14

8:00pm.

Seriously bothered? Isaiah 43: 1-2. Really good stuff, take it to heart. Take this with you no matter where you are going. God understands you when no one else does. Especially when we end up in rushing water for the fiercest fires of life. Be thankful. Just let Him BE in your heart. I hope you understand and have a great week!

6-20-14

8:25pm.

Ask...seek....knock. Matt 7:7-12. What do we ask for? What should we ask for? We seek who or what? More important is "seek for who or what,why" ? And Knock on just any door? Nope knock on the right door! Life is so filled with choices. Only His promises give us clarity of heart to know what we need, know where He is and to approach Him with faith and love. It's good stuff when He's first and we're not. Hope you understand. My sermon Sunday " Ask, Seek, Knock ..."

5-18-14

9:47pm.

Special times bring special memories. First grade then high school graduation then life arrives whether it's work or college, we were pretty much ready. Friends made the whole thing easier. Homework, growing up, learning who we are, helping, forgiving, laughing and crying. I know a lotta fun along the way did help. GHS Class of 74 is having our 40th Class Reunion in July. If you've not signed up, I sure wish you would. I don't think we've finished yet, there is still a lotta fun and all that other stuff is still out there, just ahead. My friends still make it easier.

5-22-14

7:59pm.

Life, Liberty and Happiness. Seems that is not so far away when we stay close to God. Life in Him reminds us of what truly matters. Liberty provided by the resurrection of Christ brings us grace and mercy which frees us from the bondage of our past. Happiness is what He has for you, specifically for you, perfectly for you in good times and not so good times. You are loved. Hope you understand.

5-17-14

9:33pm.

I guess I post too much, but it's so "right " to ask family and friends to pray for family and friends. Tonight's a little different. Say one for me. I'll be singing and preaching in the morning at Cross Roads BC at 10, will be doing a funeral @ 2 PM, tomorrow for a member of HCUC so please remember the Smiley Family. Also pray for my family as my Aunt Janice Brown passed away this afternoon. Her arrangements aren't complete. Both of these people went home peacefully and had someone in the family with them. It is so good to know that my friends and family are loving, caring, praying people. That's so much a blessing for me, very awesome indeed. Thank you.

5-12-14

8:16pm.

Life can be full of heroes, I think we all have them and they change along the journey. Mighty Mouse, Roy Rogers, Jim Hamill and Jerry Kramer, Brock Peters and everyone else, both real and imaginary, Heroes. I grew up & that was OK in my case, Music became the centerpiece of what mattered in my life. Early on I met Courtney Wilson, he was a big church pastor, sharing grace and pardon thru Christ. I was a country kid playing the piano and singing with all my heart. Brother Courtney and I have done many revivals over the years, what a true Godly Man. Today his journey changed. His faith has become sight, the time came for him to really meet his maker, to hear Jesus' voice and the heavenly hosts. No telling who he's seeing for the first time and for the last time as it's a place where we'll never grow old, there will be no tears and where PERFECT LOVE abounds. kinda makes me homesick, hope you understand.

5-5-14

9:48pm.

A friend laid his father to rest today. Such a sad time, they were so clearly very close, lives intertwined as many families are and many more are not. I paid my respects and though it was obvious condolences were welcome, they still couldn't provide what I wanted for my friend. Leaving that gathering place I remembered sounds. The sound of my mom laughing when she was surprised and happy. I heard the sound of my own father playing a pipe organ somewhere when he was in top form. Such different places in time, different families but the sounds in our hearts bring us to places very precious and never to be forgotten. Gifts from the past, hope for the future, the songs of life and family...I love to listen.

4-29-14

8:04pm.

Acts 2nd Chapter. Sweet commitment fulfilled, purpose empowered and proof again that God is a god of second chances. Sermon this Sunday " Peter, Restored, Empowered and On a Mission ".... same happens to us...once we figure out just who we are without Him, where we are going with Him and what we can accomplish for Him.... really good stuff in His Word ... Come if you can, when you can to see us at Highland Chapel Union Church. Hope you pray with a caring and thankful heart this week. Know others are praying for you to.....don't forget that....

4-16-14

9:00pm.

As another day winds down, I am reminded that He is able to keep that which I've committed unto Him when the day comes that He comes again. So the Spirit abides with us, guides us. If you don't pray much; I wish you would, so many needs and it would do you good. Now if you do pray, please ask Him to touch the untouchable, heal the hopeless, find the lost and give peace and comfort where fear and doubt prevail. As another day winds down we have a new opportunity to just love one another and a simple prayer is a good start to loving one another like He said.

04-14-14

8:18pm.

Everyone knows I love to celebrate Christmas. Every year I completely enjoy the music, laughter, parades, lights, trees, decorations and so much more! I like giving and to be honest, getting a present or two. The kids are terrific when they receive their presents. Such a great time. This coming Sunday we'll celebrate something wonderful, the reason for the season is our reason for living. He is ALIVE, He does FORGIVE, He lives in our Hearts. That's the greatest gift; His love, from the time he arrived until he went home to prepare a place for his own. Oh, what a gift!

4-7-14

8:09pm.

Friends are the best, doesn't get much better than true friendship. They have your back, stick up for you, make the best listeners, give unclouded feedback when needed, will cry with you in your situation unless making fun of it is better for you. They know the difference, your friends. Lifelong friendship is a divine gift no doubt. We're truly blessed when we find our friends and even when we lose a friend, either way my heart has those memories that I share, and that makes me smile. I saw a lot of smiles this weekend. Friends real good stuff. Friends are the best. I'm blessed, really blessed.... Your friend, Jon. Hope you understand.

4-1-14

10:12pm.

Ever had a song in your head? Drives you nuts and takes a long time to get rid of it. Usually something silly like "row,row, row Your Boat" or something positive like "Don't Worry Be Happy". Ever had a song in your heart? Drives your life and never goes away, just rests along the journey. Usually something awesome like "Amazing Grace" or "Great is Thy Faithfulness". Humming? What's your heart song?

3-24-14

This morning I had the heater on, this afternoon the A/C. hot cold, cold hot. Adjust for this, that and the other. Lights on after dark, in the dark, all to make my journey more comfortable and safe. Thank God for the warmth he grants me when the temperature of my world drops or the cooling breezes that come my way when it's heated up. His light though IS CONSTANT, ever shining, leading us, making our way more clearly defined, our reasons for living sure and our ability to share an always part of life. My world isn't the only one He gives light to; really hope you understand...

3-20-14

Encountered a great question, " How do I find my faith ? ". Just took a second to encounter the answer. Talk to the Lord, every day, about everything and make it a two way conversation. Don't cut Him off with " I, Me my something " when He's communicating. Don't pick an argument because you'll lose (but you know that) take what He says to heart, holding it close, thinking about it over and over. Then tomorrow when the same question arises maybe out of a great need, just search your heart, you carry it with you all the time, use it quite often. You'll find His promises, Faith, Hope and Love. The greatest is Love of course, the other two are the real deal too when it comes to believing. Hope you understand.

3-16-15

7:30pm.

Another soldier's gone home, others in my world are waiting, held here with us by only the chains of sickness and trial. As believers hope is alive, true and factual. Tonight when you say your prayers, after the amen part, pick up your copy of His word, no matter what the initials (RSV, KJV, NKJV, HCS and others) are on the spine. It's what's in the heart of His word that speaks to ours so check out 1 Peter :3-5. Then say another one....Amen. Love imperishable, uncorrupted and unfaded .Hope you understand.

3-10-15

9:51pm.

Time to rest a while. Sometimes I wonder why I get so tired and guess it's because I need the rest. If I don't get tired I don't see the need of rest, yet it's there in its own time. Same goes for waiting on God. I try to handle so many things on my own, using what he gave me, then when I see my own frailty, falling short I remember God is there, in His time. So just like when I rest, I stop, pray and let God do what He does best in both situations and that's take care of me. I'm fearfully and wonderfully made and He's awesome, merciful and gives me grace and love.... sometimes when I don't even know it.... hope you understand.

3-6-14

9:35pm.

Thought for Sunday: John 3:8. Sometimes you simply can't explain what God does, how He does it but we always know why. As He said we can only hear the wind, whether a big deal or a soothing breeze, we're not sure where it actually comes from or where it's going. His ways are not our ways, His thoughts are not our thoughts, His love though is perfect and the older I get the more I get it.

3-4-14

What did you do today? How did you change? What did you listen for? Did God's love cross your mind? Did you hear the still small voice? Where was it coming from? Could you have done anything differently? Did someone give you a hard time? Did God's love cross your path? Did you see anything differently? Were you misunderstood today? When you stopped doing today did you have peace? Did God's love cross make a difference? Hope you understand...

2-27-14

7:46pm.

This coming Sunday's thought. Is 58:11. If you're thirsty for something more in life, read this. If you've lost your direction, read this. If you are feeling weak and helpless, read this. If your faith seems just out of reach, read this. Goes right along with Luke 10:27. I pray you have peace in your heart and kindness on your lips and encouragement all along your journey. Hope you understand.

2-25-14

10:18pm.

I have a friend who has been given some pretty bad news. I have a friend who the love of their life has been given some bad news. I care about my friends. How they love each other and have cared for each other in some tough times. I was there when they promised each to the other to take each other through life. I have another friend, He listens to us when we talk to him, share our hearts with Him. He was there when they made their promises, He's there as they keep them, would you ask Him to take away the bad news? I hope you understand.... thanks my friends... thanks

2-10:18pm.

Closed my eyes again a while ago...saw quite a lot. Saw myself in the lunch line, being told to be quiet while laughing at something with my friends, probably last names beginning with a B or C. Then I heard a baseball getting hit real good and then hearing go, go, go as someone rounded first base. In just a moment or two I heard someone softly saying, "it'll be OK ", " you'll see "...couldn't quite make out who it was... then in my next breath I found a prayer, simple and uncomplicated. Thank You Lord. I never know when He'll decide to remind me who He really is, even in an easy way like just closing my eyes. With Him though there is so much to see. Hope you understand.

2-19-14

Ever had your back to the wall? Usually that's when someone else is pushing us around. Then there's the question, seldom asked, "ever had your front to the wall?" Usually that happens when we're in control. Very difficult to admit either way. We remember that God will lead us if we let him, show us if we'll look, talk to us if we'll listen and listen to us if we'll pray. No walls with Him. Matter of fact what He opens no one can close and what He closes no one can open. Hope you understand. Keep trusting while you're adjusting while we are on our journeys.

2-15-14

Good Morning Life! I'm enjoying the day! I'll smile today! I like it when my heart hums one of the happy melodies! You don't get to hear that, I do. My sermon's ready for tomorrow and I've have reflected on how God does make a way for us, His kids, His creations. Yep, Good Morning Lord! I'm enjoying the day you've given us. A moment of contentment is a powerful thing. Hope you understand.

2-9-14

6:45pm.

We've had a wonderful day at Highland Chapel Union Church. Our SS class was great as we look at Revelations. We had many visitors today and are so glad they chose to come be with us. The music was so powerful, Garland, Sylvia and our choir did a wonderful job and God paid us a visit no doubt. We celebrate being new creations, no matter what age and how long a believer has believed, they are a new creation. The miracle of mercy and grace. His love should rule our hearts and His spirit guide our ways. We are not perfect, but forgiven. Hope you understand.

2-1-14

3:44pm.

FOCUS- it's not the hurt, it's the healing. Not the journey, it's the destination. Not the wrong, It's the right. It's not what's said but what is understood. Not the thought, it's the action. Not the out, it's the in. Not a wish but the reality of prayers being answered. This week I've seen God work in a dozen different lives, that's Him. I've seen hope in the hopelessness of life, kindness in the harsh reality of our frailty, people reaching out beyond their own capability simply because of love. God is love. Joshua 1:9. My sermon tomorrow.

1-21-14

8:00pm.

Years ago, I was around 13-14 years old and going thru one of those insecure, feel like I'm not good enough times that we have in life. I went to a retreat with our church to Camp Nor-Da -Tha.....?..... While I was there I was reminded that even when others don't understand me, my Father in heaven does. He comprehends my struggles, tolerates my whining, loves my soul and is my constant friend. I'm quite a lot older now and all He was to me back then He still is today and more. Nothing else in my life compares to His faithfulness to a country kid trying to fit into life. Without Him life is just another moving target, He fulfills that need to fit. I hope you can feel what I know.

1-13-14

8:01pm.

No matter how beautiful the sands of a beach can be or the majesty of mountain snow covered peaks or a pristine field grain waving in the wind or the wonder of a water fall or impressive views from high places or the simple appreciation of an apple blossom...nothing compares, nothing, to the beauty of the heart of a soul that's found mercy, Love and grace. No comparison. A peaceful heart is the true pinnacle of what's beautiful. Of course God did it all. For us....including the heart!

1-7-14

9:52pm.

I'm right here on the table. Been picked up a few times lately so someone could get the dusting done. The pictures of the kids and your mom and dad are still neatly, safely in my pages. The day I was given to you is written clearly on my first page. There have been times when we were very close, that's been a while. I'm not one that likes being closed up. I breathe when I'm opened up and really dig being flipped thru until we have our conversations. I love my time with you. I really love it when I know you know what's inside me, that's what I'm all about, taking care of you. I'm waiting until you need me, ready when you want comfort, direction and recall those reminders of love beyond measure. I'll always give you His words, His promises, His truth. Think of me soon and have a good day, I'm just a reach away..... love you, Bible.

1-6-14

8:17pm.

I believe that I need the Lord every day. I believe He can help me, show me, guide me, hear me, understand me, talk to me, heal me, forgive me and love me. I believe that we need the Lord every day. I believe he can change us, lead us, teach us, heal our hearts and impart peace like no other remedy. I believe that He is our hope, our promise of tomorrow beyond what we can see. He exceeds expectations if we pay attention, He gives us strength to go farther, do more and make a difference in our world beyond anything we can imagine doing on our own. After all He really IS GOD, alive and well and loving us all you know...

1-1-14

The year is new, our opportunities are many. We are all aware of our ever present challenges that require our prayers, our commitment to loving each other and seeking God's grace and wisdom. We should also set a goal. Not an impossible, setting oneself up for failure goal, but a goal. We begin reaching now. I'm convinced that we need to set spiritual goals, each one seeking and finding God's place in our lives and letting Him live there. Think about that. As we grow in that relationship, meeting that goal we've set then all the other things in our lives are improved; the good stuff gets gooder and the bad stuff gets better. Hope is hope and must thrive in His people. Get a goal and ask God to help you. He will, yes He will. He set a goal a long time ago when we gave us His Son.

12-27-13

4:11pm.

Sunday's Sermon: "Wisdom for Living ". It's the simple things that God provides that mean the most. When we seek the simple, humbly, He knows our hearts. Just as King Solomon learned with his request in a dream, God is gracious as He has a personal relationship with each of His children by knowing their heart. That means us/you/them depending on how you're thinking right now. Sometimes we do need to go back to having "faith like a child" even if it's a fight, because that's the kind of faith we really need to live. Deep down we know that's important. Blessings and come see us at Highland Chapel.

12-25-23

Merry Christmas my friends and family. Thank you for being you. Thank you for blessing my life with the gift of friendship, family fellowship and the joy of simply knowing you, counting on you and trusting you. We will continue to walk, talk, smile, cry, laugh, grieve, sing, play, pray and learn together... and that's good stuff. What a difference you make in my life!

9:56pm.

It will be Christmas Day in a while. Right now kiddos are looking up, watching the sky to see Santa, bringing presents and happiness to the world. Santa is cool. A long time ago, shepherds and wise men looked up to find hope and promises fulfilled. We should look up every day in anticipation of our Redeemer coming for His own, He said he would come from the Eastern Sky. He is awesome. Now it's difficult to look up all the time, so it helps to look down, bowing and sharing your heart with God. After all He is your Living Lord. Merry Christmas & as hard as it seems, keep looking up. He's there, all the time!

CPSIA information can be obtained at www.ICGtesting.com
Printed in the USA
LVOW11s2054220416

484932LV00001B/1/P